SNOW

BY HARRIET BRUNDLE

Weather
Explorers

Weather
Explorers

©2016
Book Life
King's Lynn
Norfolk
PE30 4LS

ISBN: 978-1-910512-74-6

Written by:
Harriet Brundle
Edited by:
Gemma McMullen
Designed by:
Drue Rintoul

A catalogue record for this book
is available from the British Library.

CONTENTS

PAGE 4   Snow

PAGE 6   How is Snow Made?

PAGE 8   Seasons of the Year

PAGE 10   Snow in Winter

PAGE 12   What do we Wear in the Snow?

PAGE 14   Plants

PAGE 16   Animals

PAGE 18   Melting Snow

PAGE 20   Things to do in the Snow

PAGE 22   Did you Know?

PAGE 24   Glossary and Index

Words in **bold** can be found
in the glossary on page 24.

SNOW

When the weather is very cold, sometimes it snows.

SNOW IS VERY COLD TO TOUCH!

If it is cold enough, the snow will stay on the ground.

HOW IS SNOW MADE?

Snow is made from water that has frozen in the sky and turned into ice.

WATER MUST BE AT 0 **degrees** IN TEMPERATURE TO FREEZE.

The ice falls from the sky in snowflakes.
When this happens, it is snowing!

SNOWFLAKE

SEASONS OF THE YEAR

There are four seasons in a year.

SPRING

SUMMER

WINTER

AUTUMN

The winter months are December, January and February.

SNOW IN WINTER

It is most likely to snow in the winter because it is the coldest season.

There are less hours of sunshine in winter than in any other season.

WHAT DO WE WEAR IN THE SNOW?

Snow is very cold so we need to stay warm. We wear gloves to keep our hands warm.

GLOVES

Snow boots keep our feet warm and stop them from getting wet.

PLANTS

Many plants cannot live in the cold snow.
They die in the Winter.

We can plant **bulbs** in the garden in the winter.
They will start to grow when the weather gets warmer.

BULB

ANIMALS

When the weather is cold, some animals will hibernate. This means they find a safe place and sleep through the winter.

Some animals live in places where there is snow all the time. Polar bears have lots of fur on their bodies to keep them warm.

POLAR BEAR

MELTING SNOW

When the sun shines on snow,
it gets warm and melts.

When snow melts it turns back into liquid water. Some of the water goes into the ground and some stays on the **surface**.

THINGS TO DO IN THE SNOW

We can make a snowman in the garden!

DON'T FORGET TO ADD HIS EYES, NOSE AND MOUTH!

It is fun to go sledging down hills in the slippery snow.

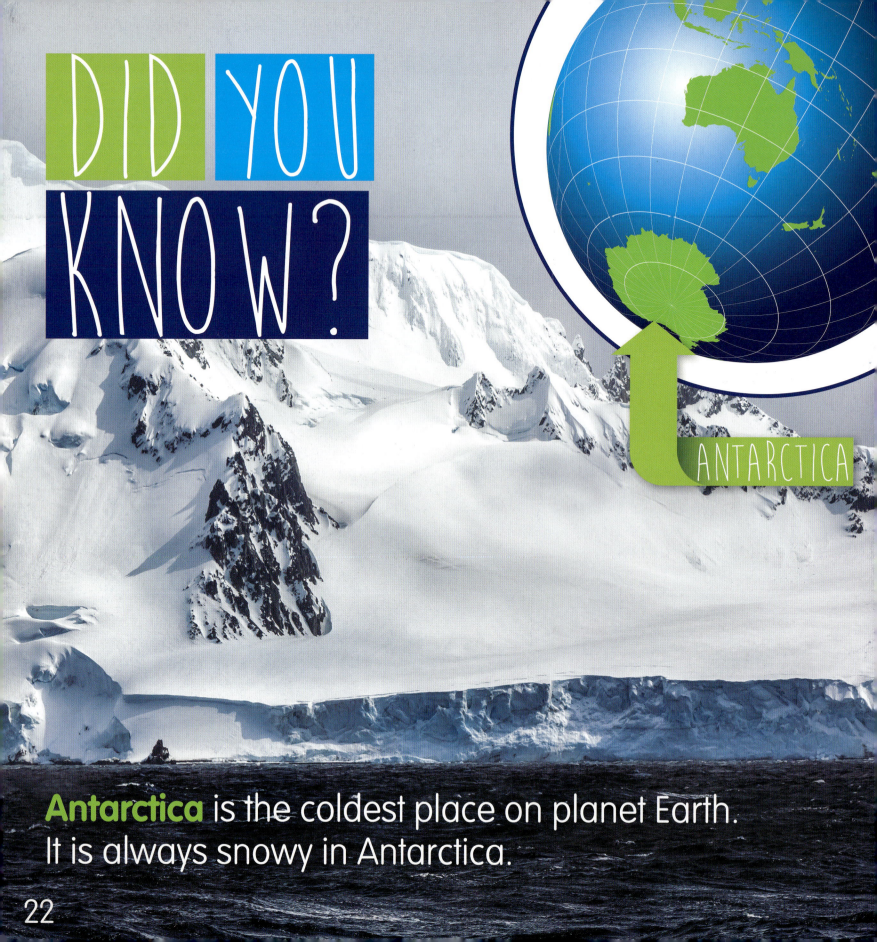

DID YOU KNOW?

ANTARCTICA

Antarctica is the coldest place on planet Earth.
It is always snowy in Antarctica.

Snow falls in snowflakes.
Each snowflake looks
different to the next.

THERE ARE
NEVER TWO THAT
LOOK EXACTLY
THE SAME.

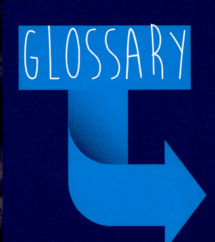

GLOSSARY

Antarctica: part of the planet on which there is always snow.

Bulb: the part that plants grow from.

Degrees: the unit we use to measure the temperature.

Surface: the top or outer part of something.

INDEX

Cold: 4, 5, 10, 12, 14, 16, 22.
Warm: 12, 13, 15, 17, 18.
Water: 6, 19.
Winter: 8, 9, 10, 11, 14, 15, 16.

CREDITS

Photocredits: Abbreviations: l-left, r-right, b-bottom, t-top, c-centre, m-middle.
All images are courtesy of Shutterstock.com.

Front Cover – mythja. 1 – mexrix. 2-3 – haveseen. 4 – Creative Travel Projects. 5 – gorillaimages. 5inset – L.F. 6 – Janis Smits. 6l – OlegDoroshin. 6inset – Serg Zastavkin. 7 – Lane V. Erickson. 7inset – Kostenko Maxim. 8tl – Drew Rawcliffe. 8tr – Sunny studio. 8bl – Steve Horsley. 8br – balounm. 9 – JonesHon. 10 – Silberkorn. 11 – Halfbottle. 11 – LilKar. 12 – ISchmidt. 13 – Vronska. 13inset – Christi Tolbert. 14 – rootstock. 15 – LianeM. 15inset – Sergii Korshun. 16 – Dmitri Gomon. 17 – Sergey Uryadnikov. 18 – Ivory27. 18inset – Photobac. 19 – Tischenko Irina. 19inset – Alex Egorov. 20 – Evgeny Bakharev. 21 – pio3. 22 – jo Crebbin. 23 – LilKar. 23inset – Jefunne. 24 – Creative Travel Projects.